It Was Important To Me

MJ Parman

BookLeaf Publishing

Presentation by *BookLeaf Publishing*

Web: www.bookleafpub.com

E-mail: info@bookleafpub.com

ISBN: 9789357210607

First edition 2022

DEDICATION

To All The Girls Who Have Lost Their Boys

ACKNOWLEDGEMENT

It is amazing how many people carry us to who we are.
Because of that, I cannot possibly credit them all adequately.

If you have pushed me to the pen, thank you.

Listening to Country

Let me paint the scene:
    Two twenty-somethings
            drunk & sweating.
One touches the other in a
novel way;
             the favor is exchanged.
She can't help but be noisy.

This is the only summer he'll
be 23
        (and it was with me).

  If this was a
         movie
he wouldn't have died.

Polite, strong hands pulling down
          on the soft white expanse
          of her waist,
lit only by the light of the television.

A pair of people, dripping
  whiskey, $2 Ziegenbocks
    open-mouth kissing.
           Drunk, laughing
               Right where both,

separately
had plotted to be.

Together.
Naked.

Happy.

13 August

Night in the parking lot
    — the electricity of the
        memory feels too loud
        to be safe to go back
        and touch—

I replay it— a live wire—

      your grin
      the bar lights going dark
          behind us
      your truck behind us
      my jiggling keys
      us both grinning

"I know what's about to happen"
      "Oh and what's that"
Here we both laugh
  —the crackle of power surging
      through how I remember
              you—

The light of the glee of
that night
        burns so bright.

Wandering

My father loathes in me
a trait venerated
in his: father
    uncles
    great-grandfather

Cowboys wander,
    and I wander, too.

He chastises me
for not settling,
when all I have is
a hope chest full of leaving.

From town to town,
job to job,
empty bottle of rye to...

all the nights looking up
into his whiskey-dark eyes
hands gripping the backs of
my thighs; telling him stories
about Spain and Germany and
Mexico, after. Seeing The Away
dance in his eyes, knowing

what he saw in me was beauty—
the leaving was a shine
buffed into me, reflecting
freedom to a young man
who had rarely seen outside of
Texas.
With him I dreamt of home
in a way that felt settling.

Horse whinnies punctuating
the night of our lives.

If I knew how to settle,
I would, but even fertile soil

grows cold.

The Love of Land

Mist melting off the pastureland
early in the morning
A barn, a dim grey amongst all the
whisps of dove colored ground clouds.

Never shall I untie love of this land
from my mind's effigy of this young man.

Art History

Bernini was notoriously unkind.
That bit about him has survived centuries.
As has his art.

Bernini's beautiful men,
bodies moving methodically.
Technically perfect.

Bernini would be humbled
to carve a saint like him for some
other scandalous altar piece, where he is
ecstasy.

Bernini would let him be a saint
that peers down upon sinners,
imperious in stone like he never is in life.

and the eyes
a brown that deserves
Da Vinci's care, or Caravaggio's,
to portray him as perhaps
Saint Augustine—
eyes so full of home and tender,
their color given truth.

A Stretch

Moments —when he is not in front of me—
I can forget how beautiful
                                        he is.

Then, before me,
                            he is stretching.
Graceful, arcing arms lifting up daily worn cap.

Lapping up the look at wine dark hair.

I delight in the
                                    level honey eyes.
                              Chiseled nose.
                              High cheekbones—
                              brought over with his family
                              from their Czech homelands
                              generations ago.

How drunk I've been on him.

To look at the face--
the kind, tender way it spake.
How gravity gets heavy when you're drunk,
the pull on your body
and there's this boy beneath me.

The at-home feeling of being near him.

A young man of many homes
and more drunk nights.

There's a town, I know, in Central Texas
where a street bears his surname.
Can you imagine?
Your family being so root-bound, that you
remember what country you come from?
(and your face shows it?)
Then, to be so woven into said small town that
there is a street called You.

Further still, the
trauma and the drama
of leaving that small place
to try to
grow somewhere
larger, where no one gives
a damn
about your last name.

Here we are, a day in August,
love drunk in his bed.
He's telling me his dog —scared of everyone,
that ran to me—
his dog doesn't kick its back leg
for anyone,

right as said back leg kicks,
for me.

With awe in his voice:
"I know everyone says this, but he doesn't do this
for anyone."

— I wonder if that's about the dog, or the man—

I smile:
"I told you, dogs like me."
Incredulity.

Am I witnessing the first time I'm too much for him?
Or was it when he told me of the felony arrest when he was 14?
He was a juvenile. Record expunged at 18.

Or perhaps,
was it when he explained to me of the family ranch.
—in that wee town where a street bears his name—
He told me how he plans to buy it back
(home tugging the corners of his eyes)

Even then.
Perhaps still the time I proved to be too much
was
when I dared to make him laugh,
tired after the bar.

Which evidence of him being comfortable
was the time that I were too much
For Him?

This is how it has always been.
            Beautiful, dark-haired boys,
            stubble on their cheeks,
            soft brown eyes—
I am either too strong at the front end in my
feelings,
or in what I say.

But more lately,
I am realizing
            that like a celestial body,
my gravity is too strong.

I pull the tide in of things they did not intend to
let slip.
            Then there I was.

                        Built for comfort:
                        listening ear,

warm soft body.
a mouth of mother's milk
advise,
that turns the trick of giving
harlot-hot kisses.

Knowing.

Gravity of being someone who just
says what I mean.

By my very nature, encouraging them,
to say what they mean,
say the things they've held so tight.

The roots that bind,
that not sixteen beers can break,
here I am listening to him say,
The home in Schulenburg…
--he intends to call it mine--

Casual Questioning

Does he save,
        just for me,
                the story of his juvenile delinquency?

Does he save,
        just for me,
                the tattoo well above his knee?

Do his friends know about
                the anxiety?

Do his friends know
                what he does to me?

Summer 2020

Nose, and hair, and plush lips,
and perpetual tan, and sturdy arms,
and square shoulders, and broad back,
and sure jaw, hands, thighs, I…

Later, those plush lips pressed against my chest
in the light of
    only one lamp.

Some way our bodies talked,
his pheromones telling mine to be
    a good girl.
    I was always convinced
    I was pregnant.

How being near him regulated
my period.
How my brain went calm with
my hand on his arm.

Fixated on his silver bracelet while
he listens to Paul and me rant
about ball & base & infielding.

He'd take me home
    and lay me down,
    and take my words away.

Perhaps his name escaping.

Putting his hands on me
    like lust
    like longing
    like need.

My breath ragged,
    my knee pushed back.

His hair, his lips, his nose
set beautifully in
    the one lamp's light.

Desperation

Lobsters are biologically immortal—
they do not grow old—
they only die of disease.
Or being killed.
    I think about this, as I move closer to your
back
    in the night.
    The bedroom without light.
    The sheets white: rustling noise in the dark.

I remove the rib
there is so much blood
I place myself into the open wound
I fill the spot left, the wound
I grow roots
I am the mandarin tree
All you eat? It sprouts from me.

Friday After Work

My foot propped on the
dark wood of his bed frame,
I explain to him— standing,
he's still laying—
what happened, and why
I am upset.
Normally he's the
one standing, talking
serious— more than
once chastising me
for disrespecting a
boundary (he's so
fiercely private. It
must be why he feels
like peace.)

I get my apology,
which I didn't think I needed,
but the relief is a Gloria in my ears.
He implies something
is changing,
and I let myself dream
of perhaps me getting
to change with him.
This kind man
who I am blessed to share a bed with.

Tears

Tears.
Tears tears tears.
Tears tears tears tears.

TEEEEEEAAAAAA
     EEEEEEAAAAAARS.
Teeeeaaaaars,
            and teaaaaaars
              and teeeeeeeeaaars

And open mouth and gulping sob and
full body shake and facial muscle spasm
ache and

   Teeaaaars
         teaarssss
            tttttteeeeeaaaaarrrsssss
  tearstearstearstearstearstearstearst…

Like a waterfall, like a watershed,
like— what is the word for the first
curtain of rain in a hurricane?

The choking of sobs a certain kind of lightning
    (tears)

gulp   gulp   gulp
teeeeeeeaaaaaars
                              tears
                                       tears

The day I learned he died,

there was a cow bellerin'
in the field—
                    probably calving.

And at his funeral,
there was a chapter full of young men
with white roses—
        white crosses pinned to their chests—
in a line to cry over his closed casket,
under a white pall.

He was home, he was field, he was cattle, he
was calm in the evenings, after loud days.

It was apparent at the funeral,
this is who he had been,
    for everyone.

I thought my years of faithful companionship
would win me some kind of raffle of his
affection—
when he was ready to put to bed
the idea of:
home and field,
cattle and calm,

with someone else.

What is a world that lets him die?

21 March

"The tiger will see you 100 times,
before you see the tiger once."

I have long thought this maxim about hunting,
about predators and prey.

With the eyes given me last morning,
I see the tiger is grief.

Or perhaps tragedy.
Stalking in the trees of potential happy
memories.

The tiger who sees my late period,
and thinks, "Let me deprive her of a baby
daddy."

Death is Never Right

Funerary norms long have
confuse me.

Who would want to see a dead body?
Much less hug and kiss it?

Then the sad, I know it to be true,
but in what way— what depth?

Now it's him set for the grave,
now all feels naturally obvious.

Of course I want to kiss him,
put my palms to his body.

A goodbye with my forehead
pressed to his— though it is miscolored.

A goodbye with my lips
pressed to his forehead—

and the profundity of sorrow.
My goodness.

Mercy

For some reason, the priest led us in
praying the Chaplet of Divine Mercy
during the Rosary

Mercy

and there I was begging
with a god I don't believe in
for

Mercy

Hurt, that now I've seen him—
he looks like himself, but not quite right—
he is truly dead, his lips wrongly dry

Mercy

This is no cruel joke,
he will not stop being dead,
simply because it pains me he is gone

Mercy

All the feelings from when

I was 24 and leaving god flood back
in a painful deluge of questioning, tears

Mercy

If you're there,
god of my youth,
how dare you take him from me, I beg

Mercy

If you're real,
you're as cruel as I thought you were
when I was the age of the dead boy, and still free

Mercy

I have never felt so bereaved
and I have seen
death

Mercy

What change is there here?
That his face, now frozen,
has lain against my thigh?

Mercy

The friendship, and the intimacy,
and my warm lips on his cold forehead,
and then no more kisses, ever again

Mercy

When the boy I loved when I turned 30
turns stiff and blue,
and his chest feels wrong when I touch him

Mercy

Sobbing through a prayer
in a room with expired love,
gasping the request that will be unmet

Mercy

Mourning Period

I awake in a pool
of my own blood,

and before my mind has time
to process the scene,
I am crying.

Like my feelings know
what my body did,
before my mind does.

What would I do
with the baby of a dead man?
Sad just the same

to be deprived
of something his,
to be called mine.

Sea of Grief

It will be a month
in six days.

A wave of sadness
so strong
it gives me seasick,
rocks any resolve I've learned
in the past 24 days.

Churning sea of grief—
the whirlpool through
open water
of despair,
the sucking emptiness
of missing him.

It opens its mouth—
a great moving maw
of deepest blue—
it drags me under,
air wrung from my lungs.

On a Tuesday,
while I'm typing.

The Path Home

It is midnight in paradise,
and the frost forming on the road
is made of diamonds.

Somewhere through the cadmium,
chrysanthemums, and chrysalis
of time— a man I would have loved, died.

Let me try to rephrase,
when he was alive,
I aimed to please and

he called me sweet and
we both knew that was a lie,
but it was ours to

build a home of for the night.

Desiderate

Kleenex by an empty bed, half drunk beer next
to it.
Eisley playing low, while the pilot light in the
oven ticks on and off.
Every pellet of shower water beading on my
exhausted skin.
No end in mind when I amble down narrow
hiking trails.

Longing thoughts: "Where did you go?"
Accusing queries wake me in the night: "Were
you ever here?"
Clustering all the desires to run my hands down
your back one more time.
Kick against pressing knowledge that I will lack
you for so much longer.

Nightmare of a Catacomb Saint

Y mi cuerpo incorruptible,
        Y mi piel. . .

Gasping awake, bolt upright.
    Bejeweled face of the saint,
        body incorrupt,
            dissolving into the night,
  leaving me with the memory
  of my dead boy
  —his now cold skin—
  in the dark of my bedroom,
  lit only by moonlight.

A Buck in the Night

Over the plot that
is your family's
— I intended to sow you
here after we'd grown old—
that stars rise, buckshot
in the 12-point night.

The darkness of the
South Central Texas sky
is profound. The South
an open wound, unhealing.
Stars weeping light
over blood-soaked ground.

You have been dead a month.
I feel less swallowed whole
by the night's wailing
gun-crack of grief,
but the stars in the sky
of my life are still hiding,
camouflaged, in the pines.

www.ingramcontent.com/pod-product-compliance
Lightning Source LLC
Chambersburg PA
CBHW051748130826
49812CB00033B/1055
9789357210607